Harmony In The House

A Family Values Model

By

David A. Stallman

**ECHOES
PRESS**

ECHOES Press - David A. Stallman

ISBN: 0970823975
ISBN 13: 9780970823977

ON PEACE and the
INDIVIDUAL SOUL

If there is light in the soul,
There will be beauty in the person.
If there is beauty in the person,
There will be harmony in the house.
If there is harmony in the house,
There will be order in the nation.
If there is order in the nation,
There will be peace in the world.

CHINESE PROVERB

Author's Note

As a new parent, there were moments of anxiety about doing the right thing for our innocent little bundle, and it seemed to get more complicated as it grew.   By our fifth child, I felt pretty confident about parenting.

This book is for the new and the experienced parent, and children of all ages. My goal is to present essential ideas in a simple and understandable model that can be an ongoing guide for families.

William Shakespeare's Hamlet is an important touchstone for me:

To your own self be true and it must follow as the night the day, you cannot then be false to any man.

PARAPHRASED FROM
SHAKESPEARE'S HAMLET

Other Published Books

David A. Stallman has written a number of publications, the most notable:

**Holmesville, Ohio – Our Home Town,
ECHOES of Topsail – Stories of the Island's Past
Women in the Wild Blue…Target-Towing
WASP at Camp Davis.**

Websites

**www.harmonyinthehouse.com
www.davidstallman.com
www.womeninthewildblue.com**

CONTENTS

CONTENTS

Introduction

A thoughtful parent or mentor fully realizes our most compelling responsibility is protecting and preparing one's child for adulthood. Living together as a family unit is a time-honored way for kids to gain a sense of belonging and security. Ideally, the family environment shows kids how to live together harmoniously, valuable preparation for living in the adult world. A family that has a clearly defined organization with values and goals assures that the family is together on what they value.

A **free society obligates us** to be moral and self-governing. Citizens living in a free society should participate in preserving their freedoms. We must respect the law, get involved in civic activities, and be individually responsible for our actions. Our children must learn to be self-governing to be prepared to assume these roles.

What I want to establish here is the importance of providing an environment that encourages individual responsibility and all the attributes consistent with living agreeably with others, and it must start with the very young. My aim is to provide a simple way for parents and children to communicate and be reminded of the principles that guide us, along with actions that have proved helpful.

The Family Model is based on the natural motivations of children and adults. It is a unique way of thinking about parenting and family harmony. By reading through the description of the Family Values Model, you will find a consistent and natural flow of values from the Personal Value System through the Family Plan and Family Handbook developed with the participation of all family members. The Family Handbook's importance to harmony cannot be overemphasized.

A life of freedom obligates us to accept responsibility. The locus of control over one's life is internal, not external. A child must develop a respectful attitude of self and others.

PARAPHRASED FROM "THE PSYCHOLOGICAL REQUIREMENTS OF A FREE SOCIETY"
EDITH PACKER, PSYCHOLOGIST

For your additional reading, see the Essays and Articles Section.

Harmony in the House

You look into our home and a rather typical evening of individual activities is in progress. Scott 17 is downstairs watching a mystery on TV. Mom, Dad and Jane, 10 are watching a comedy. Katherine 7 appears at the door waving her Family Plan and says, "We need to have a family meeting."

"The family rules say that our room is private and if we don't want someone to come in they have to respect that. Jane came in my room and took her shorts and I was still using them. I'm old enough to have a lock on my door," she said. Dad agreed that Jane had violated the rules, but Katherine should have returned her shorts voluntarily. Dad reminded them that locks on doors are not necessary if we all respect the family privacy rules.

What happened here? You see that our youngest child was able to back up her argument because the family had agreed to a set of values. Despite her position as youngest, she could hold her own with older siblings and with her parents. Everyone was reminded of their commitments to the family plan and the air was cleared.

You can see how communication and harmony can be achieved when you have a Family Plan. By following through the process the expectations of family members are clear, and because of their sense of ownership it is their Family Plan. Your child's nature is accommodated while learning how to make decisions that are consistent with their self-interest.

Part I
The Self

Personal Value System

To your own self be true and it must follow as the night the day, you cannot then be false to any man.

PARAPHRASED FROM SHAKESPEARE'S
HAMLET

Today's youth are influenced by a myriad of choices that exposes them to many outside influences, some good, and some bad. These influences can be beyond the scope of family and makes us wonder how to help them make positive decisions. A **Personal Value System** gives a child a method for thinking about right choices.

Your child's Personal Value System is the compass that provides the means for personal evaluations and choices. The simplicity of this model makes it easy to learn and use for one's entire life. Rooted in this point of view, you can work with your child in showing how to consider the options and make thoughtful choices. Most adults do this subconsciously and we need to guide our children in the process.

One's Personal Value System considers **Self-Interest, Achievements, and Relationships**, the three basic elements that give a sense of balance to our lives. This is a direct way for a parent and child to talk about making choices, tradeoffs and decisions. It can easily be shown that denying one in favor of another should be done thoughtfully. For example, if one focuses totally on **Self-Interest** and does not consider **Relationships** or **Achievement**, one's life is out of balance. A value system helps us make confident choices. Of course, the parent needs to adapt the following definitions to the child's level of understanding.

Self-Interest – Human instinct requires that we protect our life as our ultimate value. It is a powerful motivator for one's commitment to an action. All else grows from that. One's integrity requires honoring one's Self-Interest without interfering with the rights of others.

Achievements –We must give full attention to whatever we are doing, if we are to be successful. If working, give full focus to it; if studying, commit yourself to it; if involved in sports, be focused on that. Wholeheartedly engaging in our life's activities is richer and more rewarding for us.

Relationships – Earn the trust of others by always, always coming through as promised. If you cannot meet your commitment, negotiate a new one. Never violate a trust. Exchanging with others in an agreeable way develops relationships and must always foster trust. It is also in your self-interest to be helpful, agreeable, and to have compassion for others.

One's individual balance is important to feeling good about our lives. Like walking on a very narrow board, as long as you are balanced, it feels right, but if off-balance you feel awkward and try to be balanced again. In a similar way, the give and take of these three elements shows how competing interests can be considered and a thoughtful decision made. Mastering one's ability to make thoughtful choices strengthens one's self confidence and leads to a self-directed life.

Development of a child's character, confidence in self and a sense of responsibility requires ongoing guidance, building on many experiences and responses rooted in one's **Personal Value System**. This enables the development of confidence and trust in one's self, so essential to well-being.

Expectations must be spelled out to get the results you want. A clear understanding of what is expected makes correction or praise possible. Criticism must be even handed and appropriate so the child learns from it. Praise should be meaningful to both parent and child. If you over-praise, or praise when it is undeserved, it has no meaning and it undermines trust. This subject is detailed in the Essays section titled *Expectations – Praise – Criticism*.

Trust is probably the most essential value for a family. And it begins at the cradle with consistent and dependable parenting. Trust is at the heart of all meaningful relationships, and it enhances our lives, giving us confidence in ourselves and in our relationships. Trust is like a golden thread running through our lives that offers strong ties to one another, fosters positive living, and is the essence of a free society. But that thread is delicate because it can be broken by a single act and it is almost impossible to be trusted again.

The inevitable 'talk' about sex is often dreaded. But if you have a policy of open and forthright communication, you are prepared for a positive and age-appropriate discussion. Children who are self-disciplined will make good choices and act responsibly. The Personal Value System prepares the child for making choices that are responsible and in one's Self-Interest.

Definitions And Values Flow

This model provides a structure for a way of thinking and organizing choices that will become a habitual process.

Personal Value System – Defined

Self-Interest

What you want to have
What you want to do
What you want to be

Achievement

Work – Studies
Hobbies – Music – Sports
Doing one's best

Relationships

Consideration for others – Justice
Earn respect and trust
Positive/fair exchanging

The following figure shows how the personal values flow to the family level, then to societal level.

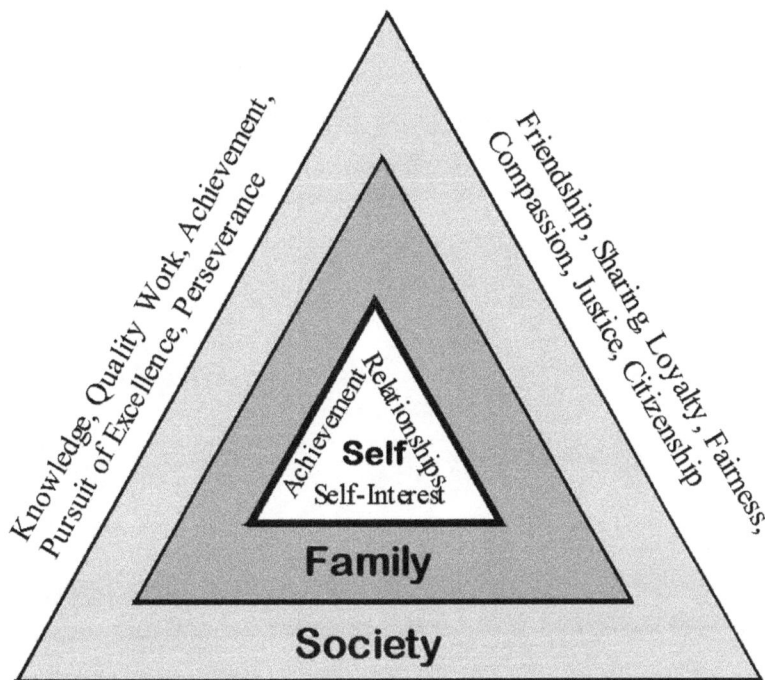

Trustworthiness, Self-discipline, Honesty, Reliability, Courage, Respectfulness, Responsibility, Accountability

Personal > Family > Society Values Flow

- **Self-Interest** – supports trustworthiness, self-discipline, honesty, respectfulness, accountability

- **Achievement** – supports knowledge, quality work, pursuit of excellence, perseverance

- **Relationships** – supports friendship, sharing, loyalty, compassion, justice, citizenship

Family Values Model

The Family Values Model is not a problem solver. Rather, the model will make problems less likely. The model serves as a guide for parenting so that a child's sense of integrity can develop naturally in family interactions. It gives your children a way of applying their personal values and developing their relationships with others.

When you show the behavior you approve of it is a powerful influence as children mimic parents. We know that kids learn what they live. It is also said that many new parents have not had the benefit of a positive parent experience. This Family Values Model can provide guidance for both parent and child.

You have here a straight-forward three part structure for communication and guidance. Age-appropriate interpretation by parents will help a younger child's understanding.

The model consists of:

- **Personal Value System**
- **Family Principles – Practices**
- **The Family Plan**

The Personal Value System provides a way to show individuals how to make choices. It can be a compass for individuals in their personal evaluation of three basic interests: **Self-Interest, Achievements and Relationships.** Further definition is in the

The Family Principles - Practices is a structure that offers day-to-day practical considerations useful in developing a harmonious family. Children will learn about being responsible for their actions and develop skills that help them in their exchanges with others. Learning to live together harmoniously prepares them for living beyond the family.

The model has a strong focus on learning how to tradeoff among competing interests to an agreeable compromise. This important skill is needed for making decisions among choices throughout one's life.

The Family Plan sums up the family values development process. Each person's goals and plans are considered in the development of the one-year plan for the family. At the same time, it enables the child to make positive choices together with the family. Everyone will have a copy of the Family Handbook that represents the agreed-to Family Plan.

Children's acceptance of parenting approaches, in large part, depends on a parent's understanding of the child's stage of development. The *Parenting - Ages and Stages*, defined by Jean Piaget, in the Essays and Articles section provides useful definitions.

Part II
The Family

Family Principles – Practices

Life is hopelessly complex for those who have no principles.

AYN RAND

The following principles have supporting practices that define them.

- **Respect yourself and act with integrity.**
- **Do your best in all you do.**
- **Care about how you live and affect others.**

Each of these principles will be described in detail with thoughts about ways to focus on them in the next three chapters.

The Family Principles - Practices are considerations for developing your Family Values. They become the daily nudges that will keep your child thinking about harmonious living. Living agreeably in a family prepares one with good habits for getting along with others.

A family socializes its children by mentoring, by educating, and by showing them how to know the adult social system. Parents should be an example of habits, attitudes, and values important to their life. Young children cannot comprehend societal values or care about issues concretely until they learn to use values as a guide for correct action. Further, children live in a "today" time horizon, so they cannot understand long-term consequences for their actions. A parent must be prepared to make the consequences of a behavior or action immediate and understood at all ages.

Your Family Principles – Practices rest on the Personal Values of everyone in the family. It is a way of supporting development of individuals in the family while promoting harmonious living. The Family Plan and Handbook chapter sums up the process.

Respect Yourself
And Act With Integrity

[A reflection on Self-Interest]

There is only one corner of the universe you can be certain of improving and that is your own self.

ALDOUS HUXLEY

Be Trustworthy:

Always come through as promised.
Be truthful, even if it is hard to do.
Be mindful of your integrity - essential to being trusted.

Practice Self-discipline:

Make plans and do them.
Be neat - Keep your stuff in order.
Do something to improve yourself each day.

Be a Good Citizen:

Clean up your mess as you go.
Do citizenship projects.
Know the law and practice justice.

An individual's integrity is an expression of one's authentic self in accord with nature. A child must develop a center of self-trust and competence to live in an uncertain world. With proper guidance and respectful attention, a child gains self-respect and personal integrity. Being truthful and positive in dealing with others, we develop trust in each other. For example, if you commit to an action and fail to do it, trust is lost and you are looked upon with suspicion. And one does lose friends if not trusted.

Justice is learned by parents being just. If you punish a child, that punishment must be reasoned and guided by principles such as "punishment fits the deed", is timely, is understood, and appropriate for the age and circumstance. Very often all that is needed is quiet time to give them time to think and settle themselves.

Katherine was a precocious child and often created a disturbance at the dinner table. We found that it was best resolved by having her leave the table to sit on the stair step and cool off. Soon she would return to the table, and all would be OK.

Everyday's focus on Family Principles integrates values that guide one's actions. A well-known Golden Rule paraphrased, 'Do to others as you would have others do to you,' is an important guide that should be a habit. I would also add that telling lies is a serious breach of trust. Parents need to help their kids discover these truths as important values to live by.

Modeling ethical behavior is an important guide to children. Honesty is confirmed when a person's wallet is found, protected and returned intact, or when a parent makes a cash purchase and returns the extra five dollar bill to a grateful clerk who made a mistake. Acts of kindness to someone in need are also noticed by the children.

Leave no tracks or clean up your own mess was a rule our family followed willingly. There is nothing as discouraging as trying to live in someone else's mess. You are more agreeable to live with, the house is cleaner and more orderly, and the family is happier if we all make it a habit to clean up as we go. Providing a place for toys and pick up after play encourages a young child to learn to keep things in order. Parents must show similar behavior.

Your children are often engaged on the Internet and in social networks. It can be a problem if kids are not thoughtful about their use of these sites. They often do not realize the consequences of careless input and need guidance. The ability to make good decisions and see consequences forms gradually and Self-Interest becomes the reliable guide.

Do Your Best In All You Do

[A Reflection on Achievements]

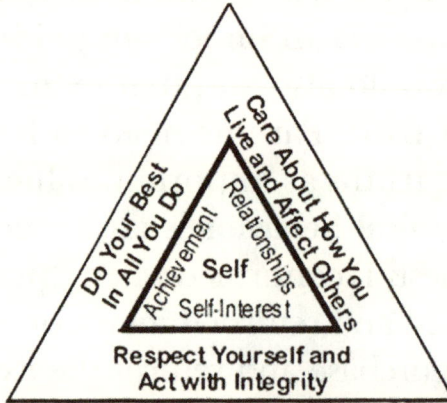

The triangle contains:
Care About How You Live and Affect Others
Do Your Best In All You Do
Achievement
Relationships
Self
Self-Interest
Respect Yourself and Act with Integrity

The products of your mind are the most precious things you own, that you possess. And you must protect them, and must not do wrong with them...

EXCERPT FROM SPEECH PROFESSOR LLEWELLYN BOLTER, BERKELEY

Know it - Be good at it - Be well educated:

Make best use of your knowledge/abilities.
Make reading and self study a habit.
Care for your body - exercise for balance.

Do quality work - It is your work - Own it:

Set goals - hold yourself accountable.
Do it right - on time - strive to be better.
Complete what you start, always.

Positive Can Do Attitude - Persevere:

Believe there is a way - don't give up.
Suggest - don't criticize.
Have a sense of humor - happy face - it's catching.

Your drive to achieve or accomplish a desired goal is another powerful motivator. This desire can take many forms and parents need to be open and help their child to follow their passion. The discoveries can be very much a part of a child's character development.

A happy and productive life requires us to relate to others in a compatible way. A child starts life thinking only of him or herself. Socializing and promoting relationships is the process of helping children know themselves and learn how to live with others in harmony. Each individual must have a coherent set of values that supports their integrity without conflict.

Being involved in school and homework is essential to holding a child's interest in learning. It demonstrates that the parents value their child's education. Kids need help in scheduling and being disciplined about homework. They should be provided a quiet place to study and rules about when study is to be done, such as no TV, sitting up in a chair with good lighting. The goal is to make study time efficient so it is done best, and your child can keep study time manageable. Working with your child on a problem or project can be a great help to their understanding. Often an attentive ear gives encouragement. Asking to see the paper after the teacher has graded it engages you and motivates your child.

My son hated homework and a brief period of tutoring, with strategies and tips on how to study made his schoolwork much more agreeable. It is most important to be attentive to their problems and stay connected with the school.

A love of reading is profoundly important since nearly all knowledge is gained by reading books, articles, and increasingly electronically. Love of reading is more likely if parents read to their young child showing that it is a part of their life. It has been demonstrated in a recent study, that when parents read to their child, during the early years, the child will be more successful.

The library can help with advice about books and magazines appropriate to the ages of your kids. Our kids liked **Discover Magazine**, younger ones loved **Highlights** magazine and years ago I liked **Popular Science**, all of which are reading opportunities.

The arts offer a similar advantage. Kids often object to museum visits particularly as teenagers, but early exposure will help familiarize them with the experience. Their studies may require it later and it certainly broadens their horizons and conversations with others.

Music and rhythm are natural instincts. They seem basic to an individual's sense of harmony and the rhythms of the world. Taking your kids to concerts exposes them to professional musicians. Regularly playing music in your home exposes kids to music early in their lives. If your child shows an interest in music, you should support that inclination. Promote their engagement in lessons and opportunities to play in the school band or orchestra. Ideally, purchasing or renting the instrument gives them ownership and additional lessons help them advance more quickly.

Whatever the level of exposure, your bringing it to your children is important. They don't even have to carry on with music; it still benefits them by being exposed to it and they often come back to it later for enjoyment.

An entrepreneurial experience is an important lesson about dealing with people beyond family. I will always credit my managing a paper route at 11 years of age with being a valuable experience. I learned that people depended on me delivering their paper on time in rain or snow. Every week I trudged the rounds to collect for them so I could pay the distributer. I saved the profits to buy a new bicycle among other things.

Newspaper routes for kids are not very available these days, but kids that have an entrepreneurial spirit can find other ventures. They should be encouraged because it is a good lesson for life. For the very young, an allowance for doing some chores can be a start. Older kids can mow lawns, babysit or do odd jobs. In the urban and modern world it is a challenge.

Engaging with your child in some sport appropriate to the child's interest and stage of development is important. Individual or team sports should be chosen according to your child's interest and ability. Either can be an important activity for body and mind development and should be supported.

We found that our kids engaged in school provided sports and we were able to expose them to skiing and bowling both of which they enjoyed into adulthood.

Focusing on conservation in these days of replaceable products seems a forgotten value. For me, I think the habit of conserving is important and I try to practice reasonable conservation. In so doing, I would point out the importance of buying quality things and taking good care of possessions. Recycling is a good way of teaching conservation that even young children can participate in.

Money Management guidance is needed for kids to understand its place in self-management. Kids should be allowed to have an income, keep track of it, and be responsible to spend wisely while saving a portion for some purpose. Parents need to show them how money saved, if they have patience, can accumulate for a larger purpose. There are suggestions for allowances in the Family Handbook.

Care About How You Live And Affect Others

[A reflection of Relationships]

Goodness of Character is the quality which makes friendship possible.
All harmony, permanence, and fidelity come from that.

CICERO – CIRCA. 60 BC

Be a Loyal Friend, Act with Compassion:

Be trustworthy in all relationships.
Stand by your friends - treasure friendships.
Share in your friend's joys and sorrows.

25

Do Family Things Together:

Participate in sports, games, activities.
Family reading - museums - concerts -music.
Have discussions at dinner or other agreeable times.

Have Respect for Others:

Allow Privacy – respect other's property.
Earn trust – trade fairly.
Be a positive communicator.

Living together can be a struggle or it can be harmonious, and harmonious living is learnable. We all know how different we are from one another, even in the same family. One child can be well ordered while another's bedroom is in utter chaos. With a sensible organization and an agreeable family plan understood by all, individuals can live harmoniously. The Family Principles – Practices give family members a consistent structure for living together.

Communication is essential to a successful family plan and at the heart of a harmonious family. Respectful communication requires everyone to talk with one another in a positive way. To the little ones, it is important to get down to their level and insist on eye contact. Dinner table conversations can be a chance for all family members to be heard.

We had an especially loquacious child who tended to dominate dinner conversation and the others didn't get a chance. Giving each child a night to have their say first was a good solution. If discussion is slow, a good way to get things started is to ask each child to tell what was good, bad and funniest that day.

A large erasable calendar board is an absolute necessity for families with kids who have many activities, an essential feature for our family. Mom and kids normally knew what was going on, but I'd come home clueless about schedules. A large display board calendar makes every activity visible to everyone. We placed ours in the kitchen where we all went by it. Kids had their own colors and were responsible to keep their schedule current. They liked posting their activities. Schedule conflicts were visible and could be resolved more easily. It was a lifesaver. Parents and children must let each other know where they will be each day.

Old fashioned common courtesy identifies a child or adult as someone who is confident, thoughtful and values others. Daily use of "please and thank you" and consideration of others with good manners become positive habits. Parents should introduce the custom of writing thank you notes for an appreciated act or gift. I believe this makes us special when we do so. George Washington said in his *Rules of Civility,* "Every action done in company ought to be done with some sign of respect to those that are present."

Many families have basic "rules of the road" that can be anything from bedtime rituals to an insistence on putting the toilet seat back down, girls live here too. We didn't always succeed, but we tried to insist on having breakfast together because after school activities kept the older kids on different schedules. Another idea that worked for us is when two kids are sharing something by cutting it into two pieces that may not divide equally, the fair way is for one to cut it and the other person chooses the first piece. This eliminates a lot of "not fair" arguments and makes each more careful of their portions.

Health and personal care is an essential part of educating kids. Regular bathing and brushing teeth are self-evident needs, but some kids need to keep a record to be sure they are doing it. For my son, tooth brushing was an issue until I posted a schedule. He liked to check it off when done. Other habits like washing hands before eating and putting soiled clothes in the dirty clothes bin often need reinforcement. It becomes your own challenge to find what works for your child and family.

Privacy is important to people living together. Granting one another privacy is part of developing trust. Each child should have some level of privacy. Since many of us grew up in shared rooms, it can be a lock box for private stuff, or a diary for secret thoughts. If a child is fortunate to have their own room, it can be a private place. The rule is that no one enters without permission. Parents should also respect that rule except in rare situations judged very serious. Ideally, by starting young you can establish an open door policy with your children. It lets everyone know, when the door is closed, that privacy is desired.

Bullying and use of force must be shunned by parental example. Parents should show reasonable ways to solve problems without force, such that they become habitual. Physical force was not allowed in our family. Some think that using bullying force will gain respect. It seems a quicker solution and they often see adults use force to get their way. Force is a strategy that is opposed to free will and is always subject to being overcome by a stronger force.

We must learn to be thoughtful and responsible when we share and trade with others. Value for value trading is important as a life-skill and we can show our kids how to think about trading fairly. It prepares one for living with others, realizing that it is just good reasoning to be caring and share with other people.

Here is a rather familiar sharing situation. Parents often, in haste, force kids to an action in overt ways. Jimmy and Sammy are preschool friends and at play get involved in a disagreement. Sammy wants Jimmy's toy and Jimmy refuses. Mom steps in and tells Jimmy to give Sammy his toy, "Stop being so selfish." Jimmy cries and gives it up. What was learned here? There was nothing about sharing, but a lesson in how force works. Using the principle of Self-Interest an agreeable trade would have Mom suggesting that Jimmy ask Sammy to trade one of his toys so they could play with each other's toy, ending the controversy in a positive way.

Cherish each other and the time the family has together. Parents should regularly impart a sense of appreciation for what their family has together. When you have the urge to say, "I love you" or some other expressions of caring, say it, don't wait. Family tragedies or unexpected events often leave these things regrettably unsaid. At an age-appropriate time it is good for kids to recognize that.

Family Activities are a good investment. We didn't do it often, but family camping with tent, means of cooking and sleeping bags is a great family experience. We vacationed at a cottage for several years which was enjoyed by all of us. It does take some planning and effort to get the gang out, but it is worth the experience. Family games such as Monopoly are great for kids of all ages playing together and learning about buying and selling at the same time.

The Family Principles – Practices are the background for defining family responsibilities. It is essential that the entire family participate in the development of the Family Plan.

Part III
Family Plan

Family Plan Implementation

The **Family Plan consists of** responsibilities
and commitments of family members to
the one-year plan. The communication
and participation of everyone is essential for the
harmonious family.

I cannot overemphasize the importance of the
family meeting. It is at the heart of clearly commu-
nicating family goals. Over time, details of the plan
may change or individuals may ask for a change. In
our house a meeting could be called by anyone at
any time. We did not want anyone to feel that our
plan could not change.

A number of general rules were established that
we agreed were needed for the running of our house.
They were set up rather arbitrarily by my wife and me
to be incorporated in the Family Plan.

Our family was committed to resolve any problems in an agreeable way. We tried to keep rules
simple and listed three goals we believed important
for a harmonious house:

- **Respectful Communication**

- **Integrity – Trust of each family member**

- **Clean up your own mess as you go**

Some Individual Requirements are spelled out in support of family living:

- **Each person is responsible for one's own area/ room.**

- **Everything is to be kept in order with clothes picked up and in drawers/closets and dirty clothes in the laundry.**

- **Each picks up one's bathroom mess, clothes and towels.**

- **Bed is to be made and your desk & personal space in order before leaving for the day. (Make it part of your morning schedule.)**

- **Each packs one's own lunch.**

More details of home and individual rules are presented in the Stallman Family Handbook Example.

Family Plan Development

Your Family Plan is developed with the participation of everyone in the family. It merges parent's family goals and responsibilities with children's goals to become a cohesive Family Plan. The process gives the opportunity to be heard and to make some choices. The outcome is an understood one-year plan that everyone agrees we will follow. This is accomplished by having a family meeting twice a year.

The Family Kickoff Meeting becomes the catalyst for assigning responsibilities and individual goal setting, and marks the beginning of a new agreement. Some responsibilities and jobs will already be assigned by parents along with a description of those tasks. Most of the responsibilities will be chosen by family members. Parents and children are all to bring their ideas to the meeting. We found that it is important that children decide their own goals, however imperfect. Parents may do a little nudging, perhaps, but they must be the child's goals. A successful meeting requires thoughtful preparation and a spirit of cooperation.

Your Family Handbook documents the agreed-to plan. Everyone gets a copy of the Family Handbook. . As a practical matter, the meeting should be followed by a review in a week to be sure everyone is together and understands the plan.

We found two important times for our meetings, September at the start of the school year, and January at the start of the New Year. The January meeting allows a chance to revise and check on how the plan is working. And there is nothing wrong with having more than the two meetings if it seems needed.

A Family Handbook example of my family goals and responsibilities is provided as a reference for your use in developing your Family Handbook. A blank handbook can be downloaded from the website:

Stallman Family
Handbook Example

CONTENTS

OUR FAMILY HANDBOOK

To your own self be true and it must follow as the night the day, you cannot then be false to any man.

PARAPHRASED FROM SHAKESPEARE'S HAMLET

Your handbook is intended as your personal guide for a way of thinking about confusing issues and making decisions that are in your Self-Interest. When you face a hard choice, consult your handbook and always remember the quotation above about being true to yourself.

The guides presented here will make your personal values clear and naturally flow to your Family Principles - Practices. With each family member respecting those principles, a harmonious house is possible and everyone benefits. The principles are repeated here as reminders.

PERSONAL VALUE SYSTEM

Here is a drawing of your Personal Value System that will show you a way of thinking about decisions that affect you. You need only consider three elements in your thinking. They are **Self-Interest**, **Achievement**, and **Relationships**. These roots are at the base of everything you do and it is important to keep them in balance to know you are making choices right for you.

Definitions

Self-Interest is what you want to do, what you want to have and what you want to be.

Achievement is your studies, work, hobbies, striving always for excellence.

Relationships need fair and agreeable negotiation, concern and sense of justice, earn respect and trust.

Every day of your life you will need to make choices and this way of thinking will help you make decisions best for you. You will be trading among self-interest, achievement and relationships.

For example, your Self-Interest believes something should be considered, but you realize that an important Relationship will be affected. Your Achievements could also be affected and need to be considered. Modifying that choice could resolve that conflict.

On the other hand, you might decide to forget it. Your ability to use this way of thinking about choices will simplify your tradeoffs and enable you to be self-confident and make good decisions.

This Personal Value System is the foundation for the Family Value System. Each member brings their values to the family and the group develops its family sense of harmony. Your Personal Values merge with others in the family to help us work and live together happily.

FAMILY PRINCIPLES - PRACTICES

Living together can be a struggle or it can be harmonious. Living harmoniously depends on family purposes made clear by good communication and the cooperation of all family members. Structuring family principles and goals gives family members a common understanding of the family plan.

The Family Principles – Practices rest on the Personal Values of everyone in the family. These principles provide a means for cooperation and harmony among family members. The principles that bring us together are:

Respect Yourself and Act With Integrity
Do Your Best in All You Do
Care About How You Live and Affect Others

The Personal Values interact with Family Principles – Practices as shown in this display.

Focusing on Family Principles - Practices gives our family common purpose leading to harmonious living. These aims and ideas will promote a secure and happy family that can enjoy closer relationships. As these ideas become habit you will find that your relationships outside the family can be more enjoyable too.

– **Respect Self and Act With Integrity**
   [A reflection of Self-Interest]

   Be Trustworthy:
      Always come through as promised.
      Be truthful, even if it is hard to do.
      Mindful of your integrity & trust.

   Practice Self-Discipline:
      Make plans and do them.
      Be neat - Keep your stuff in order.
      Do something to improve yourself each day.

   Be a Good Citizen:
      Clean up your mess as you go.
      Do citizenship projects.
      Know the law and practice justice.

– **Do Your Best in All You Do**
   [A reflection of Achievement]

   Know it - Be good at it –Learn all you can:
      Make best use of your knowledge/abilities.

Make reading and self study a habit.
Care for your body - exercise for balance.

Quality work - It is your work - Own it:
Set goals - hold yourself accountable.
Do it right - on time - strive to be better.
Complete what you start.

Positive 'Can Do' Attitude - Persevere:
Believe there is a way - don't give up.
Suggest - don't criticize.
Have a sense of humor - happy face - it's catching.

– **Care About How You Live and Affect Others**
[A reflection of Relationships]
Be a Loyal Friend, Act with Compassion:
Be trustworthy in all relationships.
Stand by your friends –treasure friendships.
Share in your friend's joys and sorrows.

Do Family Things Together:
Participate in sports, games, activities.
Family reading - museums - concerts - movies.
Have discussions at dinner or other times.

Have Respect for Others:
Allow Privacy– respect other's property.
Earn trust – trade fairly.
Be a positive communicator.

These Family Principles-Practices help us as we live together each day, and they provide the background for defining family responsibilities. It is essential that the entire family participate in the development of your Family Plan.

Basic Family Goals

There are several goals that are essential for family harmony that must be a part of the Family Plan.

Respectful Communication – this requires everyone to talk with one another in a positive way. Parents need to know where you are and of your activities, as do others in the family. A schedule board on which each enters one's schedule is helpful. When plans change let others know.

Integrity/Trust – always truthful and positive in our dealings with one another. Trustful behavior goes beyond family to benefit your relationships with others. If trust is lost, it is nearly impossible to restore and you are suspect.

Clean up your own mess as you go. There is nothing as discouraging as trying to live in someone else's mess. You are more agreeable to live with, the house is more pleasant, and more orderly, and the family is happier if we all make it a habit to clean up. This is a personal responsibility we must honor.

RESPONSIBILITIES AND CONSIDERATIONS

FOR THE YEAR

This set of responsibilities is a snapshot in time example of what we agreed was needed for the running of our house. They were set up rather arbitrarily by my wife and me to be incorporated in the Family Plan. These were deemed essential to our overall family harmony. Anyone may call a meeting at any time.

Expectations for us all:

Each of us will do our chores on our own.
We will cooperate to keep a nice house.
We will try to solve problems agreeably.

Individual Chores:

We are each responsible for our own room. Everything is to be kept in order with clothes picked up and in drawers/closets and dirty clothes in the laundry. Each picks up our bathroom mess, clothes and towels. Bed is to be made and your desk & personal space in order before leaving for the day. (Make it part of your morning schedule.) Each packs his own lunch.

Katherine - age 7

Dishes/Kitchen cleanup (Alternate Jane).
Set Table (Alternate with Jane).
Help fold/sort clean clothes.

Jane - age 10

Set Table (Alternate with Katherine).
Dishes /Kitchen cleanup (Alternate Katherine).
Will do own laundry.

Scott - age 17

Lawn and Driveway.
Occasional assist with meals.
Will do own laundry.

Dad

Alternate Mom when Mom not here.
Help Katherine fold/sort laundry.
Garage & Basement - clean/organize.

Mom

Meals - Shopping - Laundry - (with our help).
General house cleaning.
Alternate Dad when Dad not here.

Details to Make Responsibilities Clear:

Each person responsible to carry own plates to kitchen.
    Cleanup person:
        Unload dishwasher.
        Rinse dishes.
        Load dishwasher and run it.
        Scrub clean and dry kettles skillets etc.
        Clean out sink
         Clean table and counter tops.
        Take out trash.

Bathroom each day:

Each person to remove clothes, hang up towels.

Clean up own mess at sink, such as tooth paste stuff.

Put it in order, even if it is someone else's disorder; hopefully they will do the same for you.

If each takes care of their own 'tracks' in the bathroom we won't have to assign bathroom duty.

Bedrooms each day:

Pick up things on the floor.

Desk and other furniture kept in order for study.

Make the bed - this means so it is neat and ready for company.

If your wastebasket is overflowing, take the trash out.

Lights out and blinds up so the room can enjoy the day.

The following goals were developed individually by family members. They reflect each individual's aims, stated in their own words. The *teachable moment* in goal setting is to gently suggest how their goals should support their desires and their family philosophy. [Here is an actual example of adult and kid goals. The aim is not perfection, rather to cause focus]

Some House Rules:

Study:
> Homework is to be completed by 9:00 PM.
> Study time can be chosen, but you need it without TV. You should have time, to concentrate on learning, or just to be quiet and read. Your own desk and room should be your quiet place.

Back Home after being out:
> Back home time is negotiated by event, but generally is 10:00PM for Scott on school nights and 11:00PM on weekends. Jane and Katherine to be home no later than 9:00.

Individual Goals:

The overall goal is for us to do our best in all we do, try to be a better person, friend, and help the world be a better place.

We will each set at least 3 personal goals for ourselves.

Dad's Goals:

Family   - Work with you all to see that there is a place for your things and organize basement storage.
- Read each night with Katherine - alternate is Mom.

Self   - Write five meaningful pages each day.
- Ride the bike or run each day - maintain weight.
- Guitar practice at least 10 minutes each day.

Mom's Goals:

Family   - Prepare a family dinner at least three times/week.
- Read each night to Katherine - alternate is Dad.
- Keep up with laundry.

Self   - Make time for reading for self each day.

Jane's Goals:

Family   - Help Mom in kitchen - do one meal each week.
- Be a better sister.

Self   - Practice flute 20 minutes/day.
                - Make bed each day.
                - Organize room.

Katherine's Goals:

Family   - Try to listen better.
Self   - Do homework when I get home.
                - Get organized.
                - Stop biting nails.
                - Practice piano at least 15 minutes each day.

Scott's Goals:

Family   - Mow lawn before weekend.
                - Help Dad with projects.
Self   - Get up earlier.
                - Learn new guitar piece each week.

EARNINGS RECORD KEEPING

You will each be given a weekly allowance and you are to write down how you save and spend. It is good to know how to do this for when you are older. Scott will get $20 per week because he does the lawn work and buys his own lunch. Jane will get $10 per week and buy her lunches. Katherine will get $3 per week. With guidance, each is expected to save half your allowance for some purpose you want to save for.

Earning And Spending Record

Amount Weekly _____

Date	Paid	Spent	Balance		Date	Paid	Spent	Balance
Year					Year			
Sept.					Dec.			
Total					Total			
Oct.					Jan.			
Total					Total			
Nov.					Feb.			
Total					Total			

Date	Paid	Spent	Balance		Date	Paid	Spent	Balance
Year					Year			
Mar.					June			
Total					Total			
Apr.					July			
Total					Total			
May					Aug.			
Total					Total			

Essays and Articles

Parenting – Ages And Stages Milestones

Being familiar with the defining behaviors at a given age/stage gives the parent the opportunity to be pro-active in parenting. That is, ready not only to react to the child in a good and timely way, but to anticipate situations or behaviors. Your child needs your close observation as your expectations must be clear and appropriate to the child's ability and stage of development.

Those values impressed upon the child from birth in the safety of his own family circle will no doubt be carried into his ever-larger world.

The following are brief sketches of child developmental milestones.

Ages and Stages is an excerpt from Jean Piaget's works.

Stage I: Birth to Age 2 – Sensory Motor Stage

Child learns to move about, feed self, recognizes and relates to others, begins to know good / bad. He learns by observation and imitation. This child's world is small. The parents are the focus and the primary models for behavior of all kinds.

Stage II: Age 2 to 7 – Preoperational Stage

Child gains independence, peer relationships take on some importance, child's language and motor skills develop rapidly. Thinking is concrete. Rules become important. Child's sense of her rights leads to give and take with parents. Early preoccupation with self-image development is moving toward more interaction with peer group relationships.

Stage III: Age 7 to 12 – Concrete Operational Stage

Child starts to operate independent of family with many activities taking place outside the home. Peers become a major influence in challenging parent's authority. Child increasingly understands that actions have lasting consequences. Conflicts, friendships and loyalty in peer group - conformity reaches peak about age 12. Child has concerns about fairness.

Stage IV: Age 12 to 15 – Formal Operational Stage

Child functions as a budding adult. He can reason logically and systematically and abstract from his experiences. His parents are no longer closely heeded guides. He is becoming an independent individual living according to the virtues of self, relationships and society he learned a long time ago. Seriously testing authority, ties are loosened with family in a quest for individual freedom. Sexual experimenting begins.

Stage V: Age 16 – Beyond - Independence - it is too late, folks.

Now your child is no longer a child. They are driving and operating independently. Some are preparation for college and/or work. They are likely to be engaged in even more serious authority testing and often preoccupied with love and sexual involvements. Although apparently mature, they are often not developmentally ready to work with long-term goals and consequences.

We need to help the kids think through their choices including consequences. Parents can help kids by being an instantaneous consequence generator since kids live in the moment and do not have the experience to integrate long-range consequences into their actions until around age 20.

The Ant And The Grasshopper

An Aesop's Fable from the sixth century

In a field one summer's day a Grasshopper was hopping about, chirping and singing to its heart's content. An Ant passed by, bearing along with great toil an ear of corn he was taking to the nest.

"Why not come and chat with me," said the Grasshopper, "instead of toiling and moiling in that way?"

"I am helping to lay up food for the winter," said the Ant, "and recommend you to do the same."

"Why bother about winter?" said the Grasshopper; we have got plenty of food at present." But the Ant went on its way and continued its toil.

When the winter came the Grasshopper found itself dying of hunger, while it saw the ants distributing, every day, corn and grain from the stores they had collected in the summer.

Then the Grasshopper knew...

It is best to prepare for the days of necessity.

This sixth century story informs us about consequences of failing to act for one's own sake. Parents and children should consider the attitude of ant, its dedication to self-preservation, its energetic pursuit of work, its cooperation with other ants, and it's planning for what may be ahead. Adopting the attitude of the grasshopper allows others to control your choices.

Children Learn What They Live

If a child lives with criticism,
He learns to condemn.
If a child lives with hostility,
He learns to fight.
If a child lives with ridicule,
He learns to be shy.
If a child lives with jealousy,
He learns to feel guilty.
If a child lives with tolerance,
He learns to be patient.
If a child lives with encouragement,
He learns to appreciate.
If a child lives with praise,
He learns to appreciate.
If a child lives with fairness,
He learns justice.
If a child lives with security,
He learns to have faith.
If a child lives with approval,
He learns to like himself.

If a child lives with acceptance and friendship,
He learns to find life in the world.
From chart furnished by
DELMAR STUDIOS

Expectations – Praise – Criticism

By David Stallman

You will want your child to learn important behaviors, habits and lessons. It can be a challenge to find positive motivation that urges your child to do something you believe is important. At the same time, respecting your child's autonomy encourages learning and you need to allow your kids to fail in their own way. It is hard to let them stumble when you can save them, but they do learn from correcting their mistake, and it becomes their own victory.

Expectations and limits must be spelled out to get the results you want. A clear understanding of what is expected makes correction or praise possible. Criticism must be even handed and appropriate so the child learns from it. If you over-praise, or praise when it is undeserved, it has no meaning and undermines trust.

Love of reading is essential for learning and is useful and enjoyable for one's entire life. When parents love reading it will naturally encourage kids to read. We read to our children and made sure that reading sources such as magazines and books were available. Library programs and reading clubs also encourage reading.

You might consider some ways we used in our family to encourage learning and appropriate behavior. Toddlers can be rewarded for successfully reciting the alphabet with MnM's. My son was potty trained with MnM rewards. Another son had to be reminded constantly to brush his teeth until I made a calendar of the days in a month that he could check off when they were brushed. He liked showing his record. There are various ways you can motivate, but you must be clear about expectations and react promptly when the job is done, or the lesson is lost.

We can give older children responsibility for lawn mowing tasks or other jobs for pay added to their allowance. This carries with it the opportunity to earn more and learn about being responsible to complete a job before payment. As an entry into doing work for pay, parents must exercise "tough love" at times to insist that the job be completed before payment.

Raising children to be all they can be is a long, arduous process, requiring focus on their natural inclinations and helping them to know themselves. The importance of a constructive role model that guides children as they learn about the world and their part in it cannot be overstated. Our work starts at the cradle and continues until they leave home. I hope these ideas guide you and your children through the minefields of emotions and challenge.

Trust

By David Stallman

Trust is like a golden thread running through our lives that offers strong ties to one another, fosters positive living, and is the essence of a free society. But that thread is delicate because it can be broken by a single act.

The Merriam Webster's Dictionary defines trust as "assured reliance on the character, ability, strength or truth of something or someone."

If I had to decide on a single value that I would consider most important, in any human being, it is trustworthiness. Trust is at the heart of all meaningful relationships. And it enhances our lives giving us confidence in ourselves, in our relationships, and in our society.

There are far-reaching consequences when trust is lacking, as it brings into play a defensive and negative outlook. We can live each day with the peaceful notion that we can trust our neighbors, and be protected from adversity by our police, firemen, and other support systems. Or we can adopt pessimism and live in fear, suspicion, and live a life of dread, looking under the bed and over our shoulder, just in case.

I choose to be an optimist living a life of trust. But such positive living requires an ongoing personal dedication to being self-confident, honest, fair in dealing with others, and always coming through on commitments. In short, I hold that it is my imperative to be perceived that my word is my bond. That attitude is essential if we want to expect the same from others.

From Shakespeare's Hamlet, wisely stated, *"This above all: to your own self be true, and it must follow as the night the day, you cannot then be false to any man."*

Trust is derived from a number of perceptions. We count on people who exude confidence and apparent ethical motivations, such as, a firm handshake, sincerity, direct eye contact, and demonstration of caring and love, all signals that one can be trusted.

Trust must be earned and refreshed constantly as a way of life. And it all begins in the cradle. It is learned through experience and when practiced consistently, it liberates us to live our daily lives in harmony. A parent who is trusted in all she or he does will engender in a child confidence in one's self and others. In their home, no one should have to hide their money or personal possessions from other family members. If a parent models trust, it becomes part of the child's integrity to be trustworthy.

In a free society the laws can be few, if trust can be assumed. But because of human frailties and mistrust, we need the rule of law for order and conflict resolution. It grants us some confidence that others can be 'trusted' to abide by the rules of law.

We can be trustworthy models in our homes and in our dealings with others. Your initial assumption of reasonable trust in others can be liberating. Considering risks one should temper that trust until experience confirms it. When we invest in trusting, it leads to the advantages of a peaceful world.

It simply means that each represents one's self as one honestly is, and all can relate to that honesty with trust. Our defenses can be minimized and expectations are clearly understood.

How much easier and more agreeable it would be if we could all sense trust and confidence in ourselves, our relationships and our society. I would go so far as to say that if trust is lost...our free society is lost.

Integrity

By David Stallman

Buckminster Fuller, global philosopher and inventor said that with all his work and reflections over the years, he has come to the realization that the only possibility that can assure a positive future for our world is action based on the integrity of individuals.

You just know a person of integrity as they are comfortable in their own skin. One might be shy or outgoing but in either case they seem firmly balanced and can face any situation. Living with integrity is a way of being in the world. One living with integrity will have a positive effect on one's life and on the lives of others.

Integrity is one's make up from genetic disposition, early guidance from parents, mentors, teachers, and experience. Parents must lead by consistent actions and allow the nurtured to see values in action. A child with a well established integrity will mature into a secure adult that is authentic in one's own right.

Such a person's firm handshake means it is important to shake your hand.

The Merriam Webster's Collegiate Dictionary defines integrity:

Firm adherence to a code or standard of values.

The state of being unimpaired, soundness.

The quality of being whole or completeness.

In a human characteristic sense, I would state that a person of integrity is trusted, principled, honest, and knowable and can be counted on for reasoned action. Such a foundation gives an individual an anchor point for living and a compass for evaluation of new knowledge and experience.

Living a life of integrity people believe what you say, and integrate what you say and are confident in what you do. Integrity also assumes a willingness to continually re-examine what you think you know. Living with integrity is a way of being in the world that you can master.

The complexity of living is made simple when everyone can allow their individual integrity to function in harmony with others and nature. Individual success comes from how we deal with what we are confronted with. When a person of integrity confirms an action, it means something.

The Psychological Requirements of a Free Society

By Edith Packer

The subject of my talk today is named in the title: the psychological requirements of a free society. This is a vast subject with many ramifications. In a broad survey such as this, I have time only to touch upon many topics that deserve full lectures of their own.

It is not necessary for me to explain to this audience what a free society is, or why it is desirable. I need only to emphasize that that the government of such a society is limited to protection of the individual from the initiation of physical force. Economically it is, of course, a society of laissez-faire capitalism, the government leaves the individual free to pursue his own life and happiness.

From the point of view of the individual, this means that he alone has to make all the decisions concerning his life. He must choose and identify his values, he must make such decisions as what career he will choose, where he will live, what goods he will purchase, and so on, and his life is not planned for him at all.

Thus, the essential psychological requirement of a free society is the willingness on the part of the individual to accept responsibility for his life.

Imagine, then, that you have explained to two people what a free capitalist society is. You will find that one person regards capitalism as a wonderful framework for his life, a society in which he can pursue his happiness without being obstructed by the government. The other person capitalism as a terrible threat, as a system imposing demands he cannot meet. He is frightened, for example, by the fact that under capitalism his job would not be guaranteed to him as a "right."; the prospect of losing a job, and perhaps having to learn a new skill to find employment scares him. Having to make provision periods of illness   is equally frightening to him. He asks, "What will happen to me under capitalism if I get sick or disabled? What about my old age, who will provide for me?"

These opposite reactions to capitalism represent basically different reactions to the prospect of having to assume responsibility for one's life. If most people in a society are unwilling or afraid to accept this responsibility, a capitalist society cannot come into being, or if it somehow did come into being, it will not last. People simply will not want it.

Now the question I wish to address is how does a person become self-responsible?   And more precisely, how does he come to value and enjoy self-responsibility

Many philosophical premises combine to the development of self-responsibility in a person, such on as the proper attitude toward reason, causality, free will, honesty, and so on. It is a long list. This speech focuses on only one requirement, a requirement that is particularly psychological, and the individual's sense of personal identity.

I intend to show you that, in combination with the proper philosophical premises, a strong sense of personal identity leads to the individual becoming self-responsible, and that in turn increases the likelihood that he will want to live in a free society.

A person has a strong sense of identity when he knows what he thinks and values in the important areas of his life, and continues to pursue such values in action. One experiences a strong sense of identity as an emotional constant, which can be summed up in the feeling, "I know who I am." A person, who tells you that he has spent the last six months with a guru in India trying to find out who he is, confesses that he does not know his values and does not have a strong sense, or perhaps any sense, of personal identity.

The key to personal identity is *values*. The more developed, integrated, and intensely held are a person's values, the stronger is his sense of identity.

No one is born with a strong sense of identity. It has to be developed. Such development can be observed most dramatically in the teenage period. Teenagers are normally involved in an intense process of separating and individuating themselves from their parents, eagerly trying to find the values which will make them uniquely themselves. But the development actually starts much earlier and continues throughout life.

How does a strong sense of identity develop? I have been able to identify five general prerequisites for the development of a strong sense of identity, five factors which do not by themselves guarantee a strong sense of identity, but are necessary conditions for its development.

The first prerequisite is a certain attitude toward oneself. It is a conscious or subconscious feeling which, if it could talk would say, "I am worthy of happiness. I am worth all the trouble to find out what makes me happy and then go to achieve it." This serves as a "meta-value," a value without which you actually cannot go on to achieve your other values.

The second such factor is an attitude toward reality. A person has to be convinced that reality is comprehensible, that his mind can understand it, that life is not something to be feared and avoided, but rather something to be explored, understood, and conquered. This is a "sense of life" attitude, one which views this world as a place for adventure.

The third prerequisite is a benevolent attitude toward people. A person has to recognize that other people are not demons or some malevolent force out to destroy him, or that the world is not filled with crooks and cheats who prey upon him. A benevolent attitude toward people involves respect for other people's rationality and decency.

The fourth prerequisite for building a sense of identity one's attitude toward what I call the "locus of control" over one's life. A person must regard the locus of control over his life as internal, not external. He must feel that *he* is basically in control of the course of his life. Concretely, this attitude can be expressed in such words as "I can bring about the results that I want." Or, "I am not stuck. I can change my job. I can get out of a relationship I don't like. I can change my profession, my friends, any-thing that does not make me happy, I can change."

The fifth requirement is the self-acceptance of one's uniqueness. One's attitude on this issue is perhaps most directly connected to one's sense of identity.

A person has a particular set of attributes that are part of his nature. For instance, he is, say, five feet six inches tall, has blue eyes, has a certain level of intelligence and a certain history. If a person gets stuck in waging a war against the characteristics that nature endowed him with, he immediately strikes a blow at the development of a strong sense of identity. If he is five feet six inches tall, he cannot spend the rest of his life worrying about why he isn't six feet tall. There are people, and I have worked with many of them, who are at war with their height, their looks, and their gender. In fact, the quality in himself that a person rejects need not e one that he evaluates as negative, some of my patients are at war with their positive qualities. One patient who is truly brilliant got into trouble because he could not accept the fact that he is so intelligent. Based on some experiences that happened to him in childhood, he felt, "If I allow myself to be brilliant, I can't have friends."

One's possession o one's unique nature is something that one to accept at some point.

Now I would like to return to the second person in my opening example, the person who is afraid of self-responsibility and therefore of a free society. What attitudes is he likely to have in the five areas that I have discussed? I am sorry to say that he will most likely be in serious trouble in each area.

What about the meta-value, his attitude toward himself? He feels self-doubtful and unworthy of happiness. His attitude toward reality is that it is incomprehensible. Emotionally his sense of life, if it could talk would say, "The world is a dangerous place, disaster can strike you any minute."

Publications That Influenced Me

- *The Foundations of Morality* - Henry Hazlett
- *The Values of a Free Society* – David Kelley
- *Philosophy, Who Needs It* – Ayn Rand
- *The Fountainhead* – Ayn Rand
- *Atlas Shrugged* – Ayn Rand
- *Raising Good Kids* – Kenneth Livingston
- *Psychological Requirements of a Free Society* – Edith Packer
- *I Pencil* – Leonard Read
- *The Book of Virtues* – William Bennett
- *Ethics for a New Millennium* – Dalai Lama
- *Parent Tips for Effective, Enjoyable Parenting* – Marilyn Heins
- *Who's the Boss?* – Susan Glaser, Arthur Lavin
- *I Can and I Will* - David Kelley

Acknowledgments

I gratefully recognize the assistance and support of:

Jeanne Mullins who proposed *Harmony in the House –
A Family Values Model* as title, supporting the theme.

Pomegranate Writing Group for their assistance in critiquing the manuscript as I was developing it.

Carol Hovey, my wife, who tirelessly advised and supported me in this endeavor.

Tracy Weaver the artist who interpreted the theme with cover images and logo.

My family of five children who were my inspiration and joy throughout my parenting years.

www.ingramcontent.com/pod-product-compliance
Lightning Source LLC
Chambersburg PA
CBHW030027290326
41934CB00005B/518